Praise for

"Justin Carter's *Brazos* offers a vital portrayal of coming of age in small-town Texas, one that is both elegiac and incisive as it recalls a place where too many people, like the pecan tree planted in the family's yard, 'barely grow.' These haunting lyrics explore the disaffection of the townsfolk, particularly the white boys and men whose rage so often brims into violence. When one neighbor kills another, Carter's speaker recognizes him as a man 'who, like so many of the men / who commit violence here, // was a local: born & raised here, / a man who looked like me.' The speaker of these poems, someone who has left and changed, looks back with bewilderment and alienation, but also tenderness, especially for his friends and family left behind, as he mourns a place and a time when he could still 'pretend to belong somewhere.'"

—**Corey Marks,** author of *The Rock That Is Not a Rabbit*
and *The Radio Tree*

"In Justin Carter's powerful first book, home is a bittersweet space. He makes visible the consolations of the working-class and he slows down time with arresting details, brilliant phrasing—a lyricism that refuses to avert its gaze. Sports-watching, familial narratives, and the trapdoors of teenage-hood are rendered in unflinching and tender language. But 'there is a strangeness / in the air,' an unsettling narrow-mindedness the speaker refuses to pledge allegiance to. Carter's ability to love and to call out is transformative. Here, poetry is a path forward."

—**Eduardo C. Corral,** author of *Guillotine* and *Slow Lightning*

"*Brazos* emerges from *Brazos* as both place and spirit, mostly spirit. The physical place, like the human body, has been compromised by greed, time, stupidity, and is now an amphitheater of ghosts. How the poetry, a relentless dirge, can be so gorgeous, is testimony to the truth it is hellbent on excavating: fracking, crystal meth, Home Depot, American culture—our deadly muses—abet us as we seek 'to control our own destruction.' Carter, like Odysseus's sirens, beckons our 'old boat.' Our ears are opened, almost eager, for the moment he will grab us, tear us apart. But never fear: our fear will be 'replaced eventually / by the fog of waking.' *Brazos* is a suicide note. Irresistible, communal, decided."

—**Larissa Szporluk,** author of *Virginals*

"Justin Carter's *Brazos* brings us to the small towns of Texas, the state routes and parking lots, a Texas of memory and nostalgia, violence and beauty, 'soft skin & nights driving down dirt roads.' Here, the Brazos River fills with dead fish, silt, and forgetfulness, and the men work pipelines and petrochemical plants. Here memories of a rough childhood mix with the adult knowledge that the past is irretrievable, that 'we used to burn trash together / & now we burn nothing . . . / It rains for months. / The rain is the ghost of us.' These poems are rich and complex, nuanced and intelligent, calling up lost time so vividly. Justin Carter is a terrific poet. I will return to *Brazos* with pleasure."

—**Kevin Prufer,** author of *The Fears*

BRAZOS

BRAZOS

JUSTIN CARTER

poems

Fort Smith, Arkansas

Brazos

Cover image: *West Texas Gas Flare* by Sean Hannon,
Getty Images via Canva Pro License

Edited by Casie Dodd
Design & typography by Belle Point Press

Belle Point Press, LLC
Fort Smith, Arkansas
bellepointpress.com
editor@bellepointpress.com

Find Belle Point Press
on Facebook, Substack,
and Instagram (@bellepointpress)

Printed in the United States of America

28 27 26 25 24   1 2 3 4 5

Library of Congress Control Number: 2024937659

ISBN: 978-1-960215-22-2

BRZ/BPP32

CONTENTS

I Forced a Bot to Read 1,000 of My Poems

The deer is dead. It is a ghost
on a Texas highway.

We are in a small town.
We are ghosts in a small town.

The gun holds my father.
They pull the trigger.

There is a hurricane coming in
from the Gulf.

Everything blows away.
The ghosts too.

We used to burn trash together
& now we burn nothing.

Have you found the deer?
Have you found the father?

It rains for months.
The rain is the ghost of us.

I

My Grandfather's Football Game

Standing in front
        of the mirrored glass,
my grandfather whispered prayers

that rose up
made contact with
some plane
or star

& fell back to earth.

Then it's 2002 & he's no longer standing.

The wheelchair carries him
        into the nursing home.

*

My grandfather
sits in the lounge
& stares at the wall.

What are you doing,
        the nurse asks.

Watching the Cowboys game,
        he says

as he stares at the blank space
        before him.

If *we lose this game,*
       my grandfather says.
I'll die.

The nurse looks at him
& continues to crush pills.

Do you want to know the score,
       he says behind a cough.

*

Then it's the funeral
& nothing is said.

The sun hides
behind the sky.

*

When we sleep,
everyone is alive.

*

The nurse finishes crushing the pills.

It is Spring & then Winter.

We are placing flowers
on a gravestone
      & watching the clouds
      & the sun
      & the jet planes that dart across
         & slice everything in half.

Then we are asleep again.

Dallas has tied the game
       & is setting up a field goal.

Advice for Summer

Tell them you are gone—

when the hurricane winds blow that summer
when the mother glows with anger on the porch
        speaking in a hush to the father
        who is, himself, already gone
        sleeping inside a mystery
        his clothing missing from the cabinets
when it is midnight & you feel the stillness
        rising across your skin
when the for *sale* sign appears on the old boat

Tell them you are gone—

thank the ditches for holding their secrets
thank the pecans fallen from the tree
        that you planted
        & then watched barely grow

INSECT LIFE OF TEXAS

I don't remember which way the pine needles
  point before a storm. Which patterns

of snakes we must run from—red before black,
  black before red. But I remember

the ant hills that grew so tall they engulfed
  my grandmother's fence post.

I remember the white cedar tree taking root
  in the yard, its bold invasiveness.

Before I learned how the body fit into
  other bodies. Before I learned why

we were told not to cross the street,
  I learned there was possibility under

our feet. I learned to hope that after
  40 years of the derricks bobbing

in the South Texas dirt, we might have been missed.
  Soon, stained men dug up the yard.

They forced the cattle into long-abandoned cages.
  Winter began with construction metal.

Trees discarded as collateral. & when they found
  the oil in the neighbor's soil instead,

I remember my grandmother crying. Why.
    Why them. They had a three-story home

off in the woods. We struggled to keep the mold
    from growing all down the siding.

Rumored

That the local supermarket is haunted by my uncle's ex-wife. That when her car caught fire in the parking lot all those years ago, her spirit stayed behind. That a paranormal team came in & did some tests & determined that yes, she was there & yes, for a small fee they could get rid of her. That the hardware store by the lumberyard is shutting down at the end of the month after 50 years in one family because the new Home Depot in the next town is hurting business too much & no one wants to pay for one nail what they could pay for four down there. That some house in Shady Acres was raided & inside they found the biggest meth lab in Texas. That I used to know a guy who lived down there with his mom & they both liked meth too much & this was probably where it came from. That everyone dies somehow. That they're finally putting a Starbucks in near us, in the parking lot of the mall, 12 miles away, where the KFC used to be. That the Chinese buffet was closed for the last week—health code violations. That years ago, my grandmother rented a room in her house to a woman & her child & once they told us about the maggots in their food from there. That I didn't want to go back but did anyway because there weren't other options.

BATH SALTS

At 19 we got really into chopped & screwed music

& spent our weekends in garages, stereo blasting Big Moe,
ice chests full of the cheapest beer that someone would buy for us.

That was the summer that bath salts

ruled the nation. That a man in Miami ate his roommate's face—
& in a driveway in rural Texas I sat in the passenger seat

while my friend put a package of Blitz up his nose,

snorted off the lid of an old cookie tin where he kept loose tobacco.
I rolled a cigarette & he said *dip the tip in formaldehyde,*

a thing we'd heard in a rap song once. A thing

we weren't sure if we should do, so we didn't. That night
we set fire to three couches that we'd drug out from a house

that was condemned by the state & took turns leaping the burning frame.

But in that car, those crushed synthetics in front of me—
that was a different kind of danger. Or *a little wasp spray*

& some embalming fluid. Dust them on. Shit will make you feel good.

What, I wonder, do I want?
For my body to control its own destruction.

We ride out to the county line. A gas station with a display case marked

Not For Human Consumption & then we drive back, bags hidden
under the seat where we think his parents won't find them.

What, I wonder, *do* I want?

Self-Portrait with Missing Tooth

You bite into a breakfast taco & bite out
      with one less tooth than before.

Flour tortilla shell covered in blood—

the first loss is always the most frightening,
      no matter how small.

Tomorrow three dimes underneath your pillow.
Tomorrow a wave will wash sand against a truck

that someone left on the beach,
      an insurance scam.

The police will discover the vehicle:
      flooded, unusable, reported stolen.

Think of that word.   *Stolen.*

Think of those gaps that once
      occupied your mouth
& how as time goes, the bones
      break down again

& think of childhood—how the differences
      between each form of taking

were so small
so difficult to distinguish

Autumn Begins in West Columbia, Texas

after James Wright

In the locker room, the linebacker
fixes his eyes on the light bulb
hanging from a hook, thinks of his neck
up there with it, while the quarterback
points a finger to his skull,
pretends the thumb is a trigger
& wavers over pulling it. When James Wright
said *suicidally beautiful*, those bodies
launched together, did he mean it
this way too? Skulls cracked & cracked
against each other & the turf while
a father grills sausages on sticks
for the concession stand & isn't witness
to his son, the special teams gunner,
roaring past the 50, slamming
into the return man, & falling helpless
to the field. What quiet
is quieter than the hundreds of voices
suddenly hushed, of the other boys
as they kneel in prayer
& what's louder than the applause
when he stumbles to his feet,
takes a play off, then pops back in
at defensive back? In two years,
he'll be a darkened comet on the sidelines
somewhere in the Sun Belt,
won't make his first class on Mondays
because it's too much—the way the head

shakes & shakes. *Suicidally*
beautiful. & when the games end,
years later, watch. Watch the way
the hand keeps fumbling,
the fingers have stopped understanding
what the brain needs.

FRACKING

The stars, no longer.
The telescope my father

gave me at seven
boxed up. What do we need?

To see more than
these plumes of gas when

we look up. To know
more than brackish water.

Yesterday I kissed you
while the earth

was picked over—the soil
too bare for new growth.

First Dream, Or Self-Portrait with Fire & Pitchforks

When I think of the past,
I see everyone

shaped as they are now. In my first dream,
I'm standing behind a tree.

Spanish moss draped across it
like a quiet disease. There are men there.

A semicircle of them. Their hands
filled with fire.

That light all that permeates the dark.
I'm not sure how we got there. I remember

how the moss kept expanding.
My mother always warned me

not to play in it. That there were lice
ready to implant into my skull.

But in dreams, there is hardly a thing
capable of holding us back,

& so the moss rested inches from me
& grew into me.

& the men with the fire? Even that's
temporary. The pitchforks,

the fear. It's all replaced eventually
by the fog of waking.

BEHEADED

They find the pipefitter underneath the river bridge—

the front seat of a truck. It's been days since
he worked his last shift at Dow,

days since he took the long drive down FM 2004,
past all the signs of civilization,

days since he parked beside the boat dock
where he'd been sleeping every night.

*

Someone in the RV park
across the river
notices the truck hasn't moved
in over a week.

*

If you leave the chemical plant & head down the road he took,

you'll pass the mall & the burnt-out remnants
of the old bowling alley

& the park where the Boy Scouts hold an expo each April
& the gas station where my friends & I would buy MD 20/20

& then, for a long stretch, you'll pass nothing:
scattered houses, trees, vacant fields.

*

I watch the man's father cry on the local news.

They cut off my son's head.

*

A few years back
a website posted that
"Islamic terrorism"
had arrived
in our community.

Training camps out in the woods.

In reality,
it was a circle of trailers.

A few families
who lived there together
because they feared
living alone in this place.

*

No one took his cash,
   one man says.
They left it. They had another reason.

Or the woman who says
  I know who did this.

& all her friends know
   what she means—

but only a few have the sense
       to say no, no, no—

*

All month it rained & the river swelled
until it left its banks & kept leaving.

The waters swept over everything in the county,
homes buried in ruin.

The trailers across from where the body was found
were evacuated.

The murky waters of the Brazos joined
all the local creeks together:

something new to make us forget something else.

*

One night my friends & I & a bottle of Olde English
drove out to the wilderness to look

for a home that was supposed to be haunted.

It took us too long to realize that when
the highway was rerouted, the addresses changed

& we were looking for something that didn't exist.

We remembered, then, the rumors.
The woods. The families.

We drove in circles until we found
that cluster of homes—

& that was all it was: homes.

*

On the news today
a brief story about an arrest made

in the beheading case—

a man in his mid-30s who worked
at the plant.

A man who, like so many of the men
who commit violence here,

was a local: born & raised here,
a man who looked like me.

& this story that once captivated the town
was now met with so much silence.

Those voices that wished
something external had done this

now so mysteriously quiet.

THE LEGEND OF BRITT BAILEY

We were on County Road 45 when we saw the deer,
its body skinless, splain flat on the shoulder.

& when we saw it, all we could do was scream,
shrill & bloodless like the carcass we kept driving past,

too afraid to turn back & prove it was real.

When I was nine, the librarian told us the story
of Britt Bailey, one of the first 300 men

to settle Texas. When he died, he left his wife a will:

Bury me standing by the south fence.
Beside me, place my dog
& the gun
& at my feet, place a whiskey bottle.

My friend, looking back at the darkness, says *assume*
the deer is dead. Assume someone hit it.

I turn down the radio.

Britt's wife didn't put the whiskey at his feet.
She was afraid he wouldn't make it to heaven with it there.

& now, the librarian told us, *he wanders Bailey's Prairie,*
a ball of bouncing light, searching for the bottle—

& of course, she'd said nothing about that ghost
killing & skinning deer. Nothing about how we needed

to fear the segment of highway that bore his name,
but still we did.

Still we kept moving, wondering if each approaching headlight
would do to us what was done to the deer.

Horse Poem

In the early 90s my grandmother rented out the home beside hers to a man with a horse & not much else. $300 per month—almost a good deal to live in a place that was near collapse. I'm not sure what kind of horse he had. Domesticated, so not the wild mustang, which emerged after the reintroduction of the horse to Texas. & it wasn't the thorough-breds that our family watched on television every May, those horses that unknowingly competed for a temporary glory that would end when they lost either the next race or the one after. The horses we now call the mustang—no relation to the cars my father & I would test drive but never find the money to buy—no longer need to trace their roots back to the original Spanish horses in order to be called mustangs. They just need to be wild & on federal land. It's comforting—not needing to prove a name to have it. After the Civil War, my grandfather—a few greats back—moved from New York to Texas & changed his last name from Van Houghton to Carter. But while the mustang lineage gets to function like this—name attached without the need for documentation—things are different for the race horse, each of them kept meticulously in a book, their bloodlines traced backward. I read an article that tells me all of them descend from one of three horses, though more accurate-ly 90% of them come from only one. This too comforts me. Like the yearly Easter parties where everyone in my own bloodline would come together in one space, all of us attached to this made-up name. Like the thoroughbred's lineage, there are no surprises. We know all of us.

Drown

Because I knew the river,
              I knew what was meant

when they named it *Brazos*,   named it after
God's muddy arms.   I knew what each canal hid:

slivers of murk, dead fish floating beneath the surface—

& because I knew the disappearance of the river's mouth
        (each storm filling it with more silt)

I knew the disappearance of my own mouth—
        each year of forgetting
        each unwording of the past

& when I couldn't remember anymore

              I dived to the muddy bottom
                  & tried to drown—

It was beautiful—   the weightlessness,
It was beautiful—   the belief we could crush
                          ourselves & never need
                          to learn *regret*
                          to learn *fear.*

& when I realized my body wouldn't stay there—
that the desire to float toward the sun was too much,

I was relieved.   My mother said
                        we call this the act
                        of finding our God.

I call it   *the artistry of loss*—

  but with half-breath.
& floating   alone in the Texas heat

I want to call it *the failure to turn ourselves*
    into what we've tried so hard to be.

Grasping the bulkhead
      climbing the pier

SOME THINGS I MISS

Every bar called a *beer joint* & my uncle in a cowboy hat crooning George Jones songs on Friday nights, the drift of cigarette smoke, the small impact of pool cues. Straining my eyes in the midnight fog for a lone doe beside the road, ready to swerve away. The signs forbidding us from picking up hitchhikers near the prison & the night Seth ignored them, allowed a stranger in the car who we dropped at Buc-ee's & gave quarters for the payphone. The combination radio & can opener in my grandmother's kitchen. The fire ants who built a home along the inside wall of my bedroom & how I woke one morning to my legs covered by them, & my father pouring meat tenderizer on the spots they bit. The smell of sausage coming from underneath the bleachers on a Friday night. My high school English teacher drunk & stumbling onto the back of a golf cart at a local rodeo, the cancer not yet emerged.

CARLA, OR HOW WE SHOULD HAVE FLED FROM WIND

Texas, 1961

you of the star body   the dream sky

    that encompassed us
        in the valley of childhood

you of the last night   of the world

    bottlenecked us
        inside a lull/cave

this is a prayer   for the shore where
            everything floats

the morning ray of the Gulf
    we once thought was guidance

until it became swell   became undoing

At the County Fair

"Once again, in the pursuit of beauty, / the poem is drawn toward death"
    —Susan Yuzna

Every year, my father helped a BBQ cook-off team
make their winning sausage at the county fair.
I visited once & ended up sitting in an RV for hours
before leaving, unwelcome in the presence
of the men who worked pipelines & petrochemical plants.
I walked the fairgrounds & thought of childhood:
the alligator-shaped coaster that broke down as I rode it,
the gospel singer who played before & after the bull riding.
But it all feels so abstract now.
Walking back to the car, I checked my phone.
There was a voicemail. Justin, a voice said,
Scott is in the hospital. He isn't moving.
I drove the long way home through the emptiness
of the prairie & finally, in my driveway, cried,
silently prayed & convinced myself that might work.
Does it weaken the poem to say he lived. That all—
all—he lost were his eyes, how they turned
to empty spheres. That the first friend I really lost
was barely a friend—two years later,
an acquaintance from the coffee shop, cancer.
But that night, I felt death so close by.
& for the three months he struggled against the coma,
it moved closer. When finally he woke,
the world now only blankness, I remembered
a time I'd forgotten, an old memory become
relevant again: we were 16 & stumbling
through the fog at a local park. Scott vanished.

He sent us all a text: *find me*. We spent an hour looking,
following his clues, but we never did. Eventually,
he walked over toward us & said he'd been watching
from beneath the pavilion, his eyes tracing our every move
even while the rest of us could see nothing.

Autobiography, Late 1990s, With Balloons

The failure of flight—Icarus, Icarus,
you fall down, wings lighting
the night. Listen: there is a strangeness
in the air, a strangeness in the way
you wrote small letters, placed them
in helium & sent them up—
& they rose & they rose & they rose
until they were small dots. Vanished.
Don't think of the smallness of self.
Don't think of the notes falling down
in a field somewhere, of a cow
chewing the remnants, or a river
washing away the ink. Once, the Tigris
ran black. Once, in a dream,
your grandmother was killed
by a large ball of light. Waking
you feared she was going to die
before you realized she was already dead.
So many fears that have already happened:
the truth is nothing can stay
in flight forever. You are trying to say
we've already felt ourselves pop, trying to say
I remember, trying to think of the words
you wrote on that paper when
your teacher asked *what do you want*
to tell the dead. Those words live
somewhere else now. A memory
that's close to not being a memory.
Each failed letter. Each winged fire.

WHAT THE BRAZOS PROVIDES

There's a limit
to what can be taken
from the water:

hulks of redfish
in the cooler, none
the proper size

& more of them
than we're supposed
to have anyway.

My father says
he sees the game warden
in the distance.

He ditches
his open beer can
into the river.

*

We hooked our fingers
on the hooks.

Had a bucket
of fresh-dead shrimp

& another bucket
of not-dead worms.

I don't know if it's easier
to hold what can feel

this violence or what
has already felt it.

Across the river,
three men in a pontoon

take shots & yell, yell, yell—
my father grumbles

they'll scare the fish away
as if the hooks won't.

*

Rainwater. The way
a body fills up
until its banks

don't matter, until
boundary may as well
be *tissue paper*

or *birdskull*—so empty,
so prone to breaking.

*

The only thing worse than dying
in a strange place
is being lost at the same time
& never finding your way home,

the county sheriff said
when the man's body appeared
washed onto the bank.

What becomes part of the river?

Everything inside the river.

The game warden circles back around
& more beers go into the water
& then into the fish
who are already swollen
with beer
& blood
& the skin of the dead man.

*

What do you miss?

    The way we angled down the ramps. The brackish water
    waiting to receive us.

What do you miss?

    The engine never starting the first time. My father cranking
    it over & over.

What do you miss?

    The wake. How we hit it so hard. How we almost capsized
    each time.

*

When someone gets
too fucked up,

we say one day we'll find them
floating down the Brazos,

their body an empty husk
among the debris:

the amber bottles
& downed branches
& rusted canoes
& what's left of an old trailer
        that washed up
        on the shore
        of a vacant lot

*

The silt blocked the river's mouth
until the river had no mouth.

*

No friend of mine
has died under the river's current,

though a football coach
from the junior high did—leapt

into the water to save a friend
& never came back up.

Each drink of the river
is a drink of his blood.

A reminder of this:
we've all been pulled under.

*

The boys in their camo hats
continue playing Kid Rock
from their stereos.

What do we know?

Nothing.

Not the way the sun
turns the skin red
or the way the wind
does the same thing.

But we pretend to know.

The boys in their pontoon
throw empty Bud Lights
into the river.

*It's going to scare
the goddamn fish away.*

Y'ALL

Nothing more beautiful than the blackbirds descending into the CVS parking lot every night as the sun sinks behind the horizon, as its light meshes with the glow of the chemical plant flares to create something so unique to this space. We are brought together by place & reside there under our shared illusions. In the fifth grade mock election, I didn't know if I should vote for Ralph Nader, who I knew only for how he pioneered seatbelt safety, or George W. Bush. *Bush is from Texas,* someone reminded me as I walked up to the voting sheet & I knew there was only one choice I was allowed to make—there was no room for my indecision. After the election, my father bought 10 copies of the local newspaper in case the recount changed the results, thought that reselling them could be a shortcut to wealth. Four years later, I'd repeat the advice—*he's from Texas*—to my drama class & would learn about this fallacy: that just because our lungs are full of the same dirt, we are not the same—that there's this gulf between the classes that can't be bridged by the word *y'all.* Now, I listen to a friend tell me that someone in a truck threw a can at his head as he rode his bicycle to the polling place & screamed *no Hillary voters here.* I don't know if the birds descended into the parking lot that night. Or I do know—nature doesn't stop, doesn't understand the way the world becomes forever fractured—but I want to write that they didn't, or that if they did, only some of us could still see the beauty.

ELEGY FOR PECAN TREE

We bought it one summer,
at a roadside stand near Austin—
twig-sized, leafless.

We placed it in the middle
of the yard, waited
for it to bloom—

a wait that drug on until,
years later, the first harvest
fell to the ground.

By then, though, my father
had found a new home
at which to gather pecans.

No more *we* to need these—
the squirrels carried
them all away, a gesture

I tried to read as a way
of making things useful
that would otherwise

have been forgotten,
but I couldn't.
Instead, there was just

a tree, bloomed years
after we'd needed it to.

Talisman

after Robert Rauschenberg

In the dining room,
my father—tanned
from pipeline work
& still young—
clutches a signed ball,
listens to the radio
& the announcer,
each strike bringing him
further & further
from his dream—
until it's over,
so suddenly he doesn't
know what comes next.
In Houston, there
are tears. What to do
with sadness?
& 19 years later,
my own self clutching
a different signed ball,
I watch a small screen
while we go down
in four straight games.
Why do we place
such faith in tradition?
Even now I wear
the same jersey each night
& blame losing on

how I forgot to wear it,
like my body communes
directly with a spirit that
determines these things.

All the Times My Hometown Was on the Houston News

There was the time our mayor tried to ban the n-word, a thing he argued was about stopping racism but was really an attempt to police blackness in our community, of trying to restrict language he couldn't participate in. After this, the stations returned to report on his attempt to ban sagging pants, then again when he succeeded with an ordinance to ensure music from inside a car couldn't be loud enough to be heard outside of a car—that time, I think, they came only because they had to know what he'd do next. The time a school bus stopped on County Road 3 & the driver walked off. The time the undercover agent busted 20 kids for dealing small amounts of marijuana at the high school. &, of course, there was the time the school board member said the talking doll she bought said *Islam is the light* when its string was pulled & the whole Baptist church came together with her & rallied against how the world had crept upon us.

BOTTLE CURVE

This is what you remember: collision—
        metal against metal, the way
the edges budged & how, lying there now,
      you want back to '93, to soft skin
        & nights driving down dirt roads
    & the desire to still be—
       breathing, you want to say,
but instead you think of all the things you wish
      she wasn't: a white cross where
        the road curves, the reason
    a man is spending 15 to 20 in Huntsville.
      Now, you become each thing
he took away from you: bottles of Old Milwaukee
      at the county fair, your '87 Ford speeding
        down a highway. Repetition
    won't bring you a return—remember
        the ghosts singing Hank Williams,
the answer to one impact begging to be another.

The Whining Cave

There were ceramic horses painted like the Texas flag—star across one eye—& a restaurant where my grandmother dined with Holmes Weems a week before his son-in-law killed him. There were two wooden stands in town—one sold only coffee & brisket, the other tacos. In Sweeny, the river is cloaked in mud. At night, we drank cheap beer in the back of a friend's rent house, a place we nicknamed *The Whining Cave* because the previous owner had left the back bedroom in disarray—in one corner was a broken toilet, in the other a bucket to catch rainwater, & on the walls were drawings from—we hoped—a child: scrunched, hairless faces with the words *Do Not Whine You Will Be Fine* written beside them in red crayon. Outside the house, when we'd get up at 4 a.m. to walk to the kolache shop, we'd always walk past the barber, up & washing his car, & he'd ask if he could shave my beard off or if I'd rather do it myself. For fun, we spray-painted *Not Meth* on abandoned homes & hoped the cops would waste their time looking inside.

ELEGIES

Like the nights you stopped off
at the bar & didn't make it home,
slept on your brother's lawn
or your cousin's lawn or in a ditch
because no one would let you
sleep on their lawn—missed
your day shift at the milk farm
& ended up bartending
for free beer. You blamed
everything on when you
were 14 & went with your father
to help him cook chili
at the volunteer fire department
& you & Ralph snuck outside,
dumped two beers into the grass
& filled the bottles with rocks.
Ralph put them in the street
& you hid in the bed
of your dad's Silverado until
a car zoomed through, hit
the bottle, the rocks flying up
& cracking holes
in the windshield. Everything traced
to small moments, these little elegies
for what you've become. When
you jumped from the river bridge
that long night in December,
did you know of the four who went,
only three of you would swim back?
& in the dark, you'd call his name
loud enough he might hear it,
quiet enough the cops wouldn't.

WATCHING THE 2001 DAYTONA 500 WITH MY FATHER

What, I wonder, would Baudrillard say
about the mediation of death, how millions
huddled around their televisions

& saw, not knowing then, a man
turned to blood & bone as his car
impacted the wall. It was real & it was,

in a way, not. When, later that night,
my father & I watched the news conference
where they said *we've lost Dale Earnhardt,*

did we know already that we
were now bound to the thing for life?
That we'd never watched a race before

but it would be years before we missed another:
it was the first time I had seen
someone die & though I didn't want to see

anyone else perish, I felt this responsibility,
felt I had to keep watching the spectacle because
it was part of me now. We would learn

a new vocabulary together: sway bars, restrictor plates.
That, like a crew taping sheet metal in the garage,
we'd been rebuilt—drawn to watching danger.

I remember everything about the race now.
20 cars wrecking near the middle of it,
one of them floating high above the rest

& yet everyone was fine. & then how
that final moment looked so routine, like
nothing would go wrong until it did.

My father drinking Bud Light. My aunt
with a cigarette, nervous because
she lived a few miles from Dale.

There were pork ribs, cooked
overnight on the pit. They would have
fallen apart in your hands.

SELF-PORTRAIT WITH BONFIRE

Here, the body exists
as burnt logs, as butane
leaked across the grass.
Ignite, the skin says
to the illegible sky.
There are seven ways
to cross between streets.
A dirt bike ramp made
of cow skulls. A tire swing
attached to pine needles.
Five cardinal directions
from one space to the next.
When we were young
& still fraught with heat,
the bonfire collapsed, rolled
us nearly to death. Listen
when the winds cry foul,
when smoke pushes you
against dream. Which
ash sings of violence
is a question the grass
does not want answered.

HOMESTEAD

I. This forest will push back.
Here are three fingers

cut from a hand. Here
are the missing electrons.

Q: Is a regret old skin?
A: old skin is filled

with the rigors of giving.
Make. Make a love new.

Here is the fresh couplet,
these shared organs.

Here is the prairie fire
that brings us new leaves.

II.   Father: gather bones & prayers,
       fresh kindling—set flame

       to the adventure that once
       consumed you. Take a wife

       & marry under the eyes of God
       & the county sheriff, honeymoon

       in that same beach motel where later
       you'll take the wrong body.

       For now, though, worry only
       about fidelity & childbirth.

       For now, when a God's voice
       crackles from the coals

       of a BBQ pit, listen. Keep smoking
       the chicken. Keep

       falling asleep in the same bed
       night after night after night.

III.   Last evening, lighting
        a cigar,

        your mouth thanked
        the loneliness.

        You'd rather be inside
        her voice,

        but the sky is cold,
        it has no mouth.

        They call this
        monogamy, but

        the wind changes it to
        I let it go.

IV.   He learned a trade, found a job
        climbing to the top of phone towers

        & cutting wires. We call this his
        working period—sure,

        some nights he arrived so late
        smelling of Miller Lite & motor oil,

        out too long with the co-workers,
        but he always made it back—always

        in Place A when he needed to be,
        but sometimes couldn't make it

        to Place B on time, sometimes
        would call & whisper about the truck

        not starting, how he'd be just
        a little bit & *go ahead*

        to your brother's place without me—
        & by midnight, the driveway still empty,

        he'd finally arrive, shuffle to bed
        without waking the home.

        A complicated time: his eyes
        drifting between the cross

        & his cell phone, ringing
        with the wrong numbers.

V.   How much longer until
she knows your breath,

knows the smell of wine
& sadness it carries,

the way your body ached,
so long, for the new other.

& what will she whisper
when one hand covers

the mouth, when the other
reaches inside it.

VI.   She will ask you what
you have learned & you will say

I have learned you.
I have learned how your skin

streaks across sky. Do not allow
yourself to be caught in the lie

that, somewhere, there exists
a bloodless infidelity—no,

you must watch now as she spins
needles across her fingers,

turns you to *parlor trick*,
to *observer.* But remember to listen—

her voice, this dying thing,
& the sounds of the sons, the daughter

asleep in her bedroom. Remember
the seven-letter word for why

you can never fit together the way
you want. Hint: it begins h, ends -*band*.

VII.   Heavy snow, black flowers curl
        in the tin light of the porch.

        The opening of the door, the daughters
        late again. The night, spiderwebs,

        the essence of oxen bedded
        in fresh straw. Ankle-ice.

        My dear, you wear no socks
        in spite of this wind, why?

        Come, watch the red-brick
        of the fireplace, find the long coat

        you wore until branches tore apart
        the seams. What can be fixed

        by desire? Instead of giving you
        a lie, take this false moon & swallow.

        Instead of painting globes on your nails,
        take a coal & let it spark, fire-eyed.

VIII.   The Lord asks *stay*.
The Lord asks & he listens,

keeps listening.
The Lord asks *stay*

& eventually his ears
fill with wax, eventually

he's a body on the dunes,
a body buried in the sand

with something wrong
beside him. The Lord asks *stay*

& he never hears it—
& when he leaves,

he takes only what fits
in stolen grocery carts.

Leave the rest. The Lord
asks *stay* & the answer

is to let the objects stay.
There is no word for the place

we scrub & scrub
from our memory, only

to find it never
gets washed away.

IX.   How he'd wanted his eyes
        to vanish, his skin to become

        inexplicable. That night,
        as they tore themselves apart

        on the Blue Water Highway,
        their bodies begged the road:

        don't end. & at the beachside bar
        he told her about Jeff,

        the previous owner—how he'd killed
        his wife out back. *So this,*

        he said. *Us. It isn't that bad.*
        Isn't most love a little fucked up?

        & so what if every night they left town
        for dinner, to avoid the faces

        who remembered the other
        he'd once pressed into—so what

        if the wedding is attended only
        by whispers.

IV

Dirt

Rust haloed
the gas tank.

Dusty: this town
& all the trucks

that pile up
in the junkyard.

What's morning
& what does it say

about mourning?
How much sun

can the sky take
before it gives up?

This isn't prayer.
How do you kneel

for anything other
than selfishness?

Slow Erosion

Last season, the beach moved in three more feet, the houses built on stilts above the grass now above the sand instead &, one day, above the water. The ships roll into the Intracoastal carrying oil from offshore while a father & son stand out on the rocks & cast lines into the Gulf. *The best fishing, the father says, is when the boats roar everything up.* In the distance, a truck makes circles in the sand. There's a bonfire despite the burn ban, the smoke drifting up & stopping in the middle of the air, suspended.

In the Country We'd Lost

The locomotive sings the cracked air,
a hurl of noise, of mystery. Sitting here
in the dirty truck, I wonder how the world looks.

Perhaps it's like this: a half-shadow,
an unknown motion
against these gathered storm clouds.

A lonesomeness here. Universe adrift
inside the rubble. The train finally passes:
more thunder, more thunder.

I make a metaphor of whatever I can.
Orange glow of headlights, streaks
of last week's chili on a floorboard napkin.

There's something wrong outside.
All we have though is this hope
it won't last long. Not too long.

Tonight, I need you like teeth
need something solid. Tonight,
we fight the growing dark

with these words. Electricity
only works until the next bill comes;
understanding only while the train roars.

Trash Fires

We could be doing meth &, Russell said, *nothing about this scene would be differ-ent.* The fires we set inside buckets, fueled by gasoline & old magazines. The boombox we blared rap music from. Someone tries to twerk while drinking hard cider & spills the bottle all over his shirt, so he takes it off & keeps dancing. We had three colors of spray paint & used them to draw three different penises on the barn's wall. Russell said, *I don't ever want to leave you motherfuckers.* We learned aerosol cans sound like gun-shots when burnt. We practiced safe sex by not having any. The trash fire burned old *Left Behind* novels, photographs of people we'd forgotten, a yo-yo without a string.

ALL THE PUNKS BECOME LIBERTARIANS

eventually. The ones I knew did, like
Ricky, who once shaved his head
& played guitar in an anarcho-

punk band but now does it only
as costume, a type of show—the bottles
he smashed on the garage floor

all part of an act.
One night we drank
a couple of 40s

& ended up in the backyard
shooting at squirrels. Cruelty
& stupidity mixed

together like the various alcohols
in the various punches
at the parties where we all realized

we were becoming adults differently.
How once Ricky wanted things shattered
but now wants only to destroy—

filled with ideas about gun & land
ownership. With, too,
the physicality of the gun.

& three years later the same voices
that sang Against Me!
at bonfires now have new words.

Now they're building semi-automatics
in their sheds, begging
the local congressman

to keep the refugees away. How
we all move apart. Right
& left. Away from center.

SELFIE WITH DEAD FISH

The boat ran ashore:
shallow sandbar,
mud-bottom. We were
only a mile from
what my father called
the spot, where
the Intracoastal cut over
to Matagorda Bay,
where once a tanker
sank under its own weight
& became a reef.
My father stepped out
& pushed. Engine turned.
Shale coat. Finally there,
he threw down the anchor.
Redfish reeled in every minute.
We tagged the large ones,
threw the small ones back.
When we reached the limit
we hid new ones under the old.
We put one on ice.
Never cooked it. Mounted it
above my bed, its mouth
hung open. Forever.
Eyes pointed at the window
like it wanted something
it could never have—
a way out. An escape.

MEMORY IN WHICH YOU DO NOT SPEAK

My best friend took too many bath salts & then didn't speak for 18 months. Something, his mother said, about the receptors in the brain, how they'd try to light up only to find the plug had been torn out, a wire frayed beyond repair. The first time I visited—halfway through his self-imposed exile in his stepfather's doublewide—we sat in the living room & watched half an episode of *Jeopardy*. I wondered about the way the answers were phrased as questions—if it meant something deeper. Before the episode ended, he stood up, walked toward the front door. Then I was on the back of a four-wheeler. Then I trusted myself to his silence. We sped so fast through the ditch that we became, temporarily, airborne. Became frozen—the gravel road, the horse tied to a fence in the next yard. I didn't know if I would make it back to the ground until we landed back on the ground, until he turned back toward me & smiled. After, he showed me a piece of dirt in a garden where I could tell something was trying to grow: thin, green, worming itself up from the earth. *What is it*, I asked, & for just a brief moment, the two of us alone, I expected something to eke out of his mouth—a laugh, a quiet explanation. Instead, he brought two fingers to his lips, pretended to inhale.

WE FIND A SOUP CAN FROM 1989 IN MY GRANDMOTHER'S CUPBOARD

It doesn't matter what brand it was
or if it was really green beans
or if the expiration date was 1992
& the year this happened was earlier
or later or exactly right—if it was
the year that my grandfather died
or the year my aunt moved back home
to stay with her—& it doesn't matter—
not much—that I was in a different room
& that the can was in the trash
before I even saw it & that my mother
told me about it on the drive home
& it was meant to be a funny aside
about how she'd never cleaned out
that cupboard & how the years
added up on those shelves.

New Year's Day

My parents finally depart each other
when the temperature takes
its final dive. I sit in a bar
& drink whiskey twice the price
it costs in a college town,
contemplate what coming home means
when home teeters—
when a strong wind could drive
the shingles from their place.

The house has a fresh coat of paint.
The faux wood panels turned beige.
It takes so much looking
to find any remnant of him:
an old photo of the two of us fishing
hidden behind the knick-knacks,
old burned CDs of 70s rock on a shelf.

I'll wake the morning after New Year's
to my father's vehicle outside,
to him asleep in the bed he long shared—
one final nod toward longing,
the last time I'll see them in the same room
for two years, until my rehearsal dinner.

There's a shed out back
filled with boxes of my childhood—
a Honus Wagner bobblehead,
a tub of NASCAR diecasts.
The photo album my grandmother
made for me one Christmas

when she was alive & everything
was still a kind of togetherness.

The closet where he kept his overalls
& safety glasses for work is now
where my mother sits all day
& looks at whatever the internet shows.
The office room up front
where he would do the same
is now a closet. Things tend
to shift around. A tree grows
where a different tree
once was felled by lightning.

I Go Back

In my dining room, I paced circles around the table—what I always did when the sounds of the crickets outside the window became too loud—while the stereo played the new Kenny Chesney album track by track. When "I Go Back" came on, I started to sing Mellencamp's "Jack & Diane," not aware that Chesney was about to sing *about* Mellencamp's "Jack & Diane." In that second I thought about the connections a brain makes, the way things are sometimes known before they happen, but I didn't think about what really mattered—the sentimentality of both songs, the way they ask us to remember & idealize the places we don't want to remember, the times we should just forget. The summer the Baptists kicked someone out of youth group for being gay. The summer my uncle disappeared, that my parents lied & said he was *working on the oil platforms* to avoid naming the real reasons. The summer our family drove to a small restaurant in Sargent every third Saturday for all-you-can-eat fried quail & pretended we had enough things to speak about but ended up watching sports on the muted television in the corner. The summer my grandfather's best friend died, a man named Sam whose son was, at the time, fighting to keep the family cemetery from being covered by the expansion of the highway—a fight they never could have won because the highway needed two more lanes, even though all these years later those lanes have never appeared, the state always just saying *patience, patience.* & when Chesney sings of funerals & the good dying young, I think of Casey in the back of the tractor repair yard, how he inflated a tire too much until it exploded, & of the football player who was shot outside of the county's only nightclub, & of the girl whose name I don't remember but should—how her face was turned into a decal that graced the back of every truck window in town.

What We Can't Leave Behind

Bullet holes pinged in a Coke can
in my grandmother's driveway.

The crisp smell of snow that one time
it fell from the South Texas sky.

I am a child of this river, this heat—
of these fields of crabgrass & manure.

Still, I moved. I spent two years
in a state with four letters & three vowels.

Learned ice & cold as the usual:
how it made mountains in parking lots.

Something felt more open that way—
something about the world & possibility.

I could see seasons. I could envision
a world so other than my youth.

Why must we always dwell
on those old days. On funerals.

On blood-strewn deer hanging
in the warm, winter garage.

There was always the crack
of rifles in the distance.

Self-Portrait without Adornment

Sometimes the image is only a mask.
Sometimes the town is just the town:
1500 people, a river, a grocery store where
you pay more for produce than in the city
& call it convenience. Sometimes,
I like to imagine myself still there
but it's been nearly a decade now. I visit
for holidays & leave again,
a tourist in a world of familiarity.
Self-portrait as endless train.
Years ago, an electronic billboard
advertised the fireplace store
& the boat repair shop. But one morning,
I looked up & saw Barack Obama's face
behind prison bars. I knew, then,
I needed to escape. *Self-portrait*
as lightning that never reaches the ground.
There's a shop that used to sell old clothes,
electronics; now, their yard is filled
with "Lock Her Up" signs.
The old bank is a gun store. But this
is everywhere, this feeling that home
has been hijacked. Nothing is unique—
yesterday, in a different town, I saw a poster
for a concealed carry class just for pastors.
I'll never really return to this place:
I'm 32 & know I've seen my parents
more in the past than I will
in the future. There used to be a tree
in my grandmother's yard. It fell down

in the 90s but kept growing sideways.
*Self-portrait as a ruined thing striving
to live.* Sometimes I wish I could
go back to those days & linger there
forever: a time when I could still
pretend to belong somewhere. *Self-
portrait as a tree finally hauled away.*

ACKNOWLEDGMENTS

Poems in this manuscript previously appeared in the following jour-
nals, often in slightly altered forms:

The Adroit Journal: "Drown"
Another Chicago Magazine: "Fracking"
Bad Pony: "The Legend of Britt Bailey"
Baltimore Review: "Autumn Begins in West Columbia, Texas"
Bat City Review: "Watching the 2001 Daytona 500 with my Father"
Birdfeast: "Self-Portrait with Bonfire"
Breakwater Review: "Dirt"
Cimarron Review: "Bath Salts"
The Collagist: "My Grandfather's Football Game"
Cream City Review: "Elegies"
decomP: "Homestead, III."
Gigantic Sequins: "I Go Back"
Hobart: "Bottle Curve"
Jellyfish: "Homestead, I."
The Journal: "Insect Life of Texas"
NANO Fiction: "Rumored"
New South: "Slow Erosion"
Pentimento: "Trash Fires"
Pinball: "Memory In Which You Do Not Speak"
Powder Keg: "The Whining Cave"
Prairie Schooner: "Talisman"
Reservoir: "Advice for Summer"
Scalawag: "All The Punks Become Libertarians" & "Horse Poem"
The Shore: "In The Country We'd Lost" & "We Find a Soup Can from
   1989 in My Grandmother's Cupboard"
Sonora Review: "Autobiography, Late 1990s, With Balloons"
South Carolina Review: "Self-Portrait with Missing Tooth"
Sycamore Review: "Elegy for Pecan Tree"
Whiskey Island: "Homestead, V." & "Homestead, VI."

Thanks Kevin Prufer, Larissa Szporluk, Corey Marks, & Eduardo Corral for the kind words on this manuscript.

Thanks to all the professors who helped guide these words—Kevin, Larissa, Corey, as well as Bruce Bond, Martha Serpas, Eugene Gloria, & F. Daniel Rzicznek.

Thanks to all the classmates who've given feedback on these words, especially my Bowling Green cohort—Dan, Brett, Casey.

Thanks to Casie for putting this book out into the world.

Thanks to all the friends who inspired these works, with a special shout-out to Josh, who has been there for almost 30 years & is all over these poems.

Thanks to Karissa for everything, always. These poems wouldn't exist without you. I love you.

Thanks to Callum, who did not exist yet when any of these poems were written but who does now that's it out in the world. I love you.

Thanks to everyone who is no longer around to be thanked, especially Tony Hoagland—who kicked me out of his office once & said not to come back unless I wanted to take poetry seriously—& my grandparents & Zach Doss & Lisa & Alice, whose kitchen I was sitting in when this manuscript was picked up.

JUSTIN CARTER'S poems have appeared in *The Adroit Journal*, *Bat City Review*, DIAGRAM, and other spaces. Originally from the Texas Gulf Coast, Justin currently lives in Iowa and works as a sports writer and editor. *Brazos* is his debut collection.

Belle Point Press is a literary small press along the Arkansas-Oklahoma border. Our mission is simple: Stick around and read. Learn more at **bellepointpress.com**.